Michael Paul's Discourse

The Penumbra

The Penumbra
©2014 by Michael Paul

Cover design by Breanna Frances

All rights reserved. No part of this book may be reproduced or transmitted in any form or by any means, electronic or mechanical, including photocopying, recording, or by any information storage and retrieval system, without permission from the author.

Print ISBN 978-0-9904281-4-5

New Living Translation, Tyndale House, © 1996.

Scripture quotations are taken from *The New King James Version*. Copyright ©1982 by Thomas Nelson, Inc. Used by permission. All rights reserved.

Scripture taken from *The Holy Bible, English Standard Version*. Copyright © 2000, 2001 by Crossway Bibles, a division of Good News Publishers. Used by permission. All rights reserved.

Contents

Dedication ii

Acknowledgements iii

Preface iv

Introduction v

Chapter I, Of the Origin & History 1

Chapter II, Of the Nature of Allah, Mohammed, and Jesus ... 6

Chapter III, Of the Fundamentals 12

Chapter IV, Of the Social Life & Cultural 34

Chapter V, Of the State of War & Peace 52

Conclusion 58

Resources 60

About the Author 62

Dedication

When the night comes, the roads go to sleep. Most lights go off, except the light of the home. To my new home, my new nation, the United States of America, I dedicate this book.

Michael Paul

Acknowledgements

To the beautiful spirit of my mother, who taught me the alphabet of love. She was my original cradle of love, where all time stopped and upon whose face I saw the glowing reflection of the deep Iraqi history.

and

To my first teacher, my father, who ingrained in me an unquenchable desire for reading and learning as much as possible. For all things rational in me, I thank him. I wish they both could have been here to share with me the joy in this accomplishment.

    Michael Paul

Preface

The liberal idea in the world today, claims that Christianity and Islam come from the same source. That they are two sides to the same coin. If I were to accept this claim, I would expect both teachings to contain identical moral and theological ideas. However, close examination shows unequivocally that their teachings are actually divergent and contradictory, suggesting that they do not originate from the same authority. One teaching leads to a lot of doubt and confusion, and the other does not. This analysis illustrates the enormous gap that separates their teachings. I will discuss each teaching and its key assertions. My aim behind this study is that through this journey, you will gain for yourself an understanding of the reality.

Introduction

The story of this book began almost a quarter century ago, with my "conversion." The world would call it conversion, but to me it was a return to my original, intended state of being: the Christian nature. I collected many observations over the years and went to great lengths to carry them with me to my new life in the United States, that I might use them to impact American Christians with a desire to win Muslims for the Gospel. Penumbra is the shade area of the light, a hidden, obscure area. Christianity is the source of the light, but the foundation of Islam was taken from the biblical facts and reshaped to create the religion of Islam. My book is intended to shed light on this shady area.

When I intend to scrutinize existing, illogical, irrational principles, Voltaire's quote comes to mind, "You need a century to compound prevailing opinion." In this critical study, I am not trying to change minds or beliefs; I just want to focus on Islam as a religion, built atop the crisp, gritty foundation of the Arabian Peninsula. Mixed into that inheritance was the atmosphere of a pagan, ignorant era, prevalent on the Arab peninsula at that time. The term "Islam" means "docile, obedient and surrendered." Islamic teachings are filled with thousands, if not millions, of questions, making it similar to a very difficult crossword puzzle, impossible to figure out, even for Muslims themselves.

Confusion and doubt have slammed the door of the light, which gives the blind back their sight. The reality about Islam is there are many mazes that lead man into uncertainty. In point of fact, questioning is the key to the door of certainty.

Is Islam the religion of truth?

Is Islam a religion from the God?

In this challenging study, I have contributed for the development of humanity, to stimulate the mind of the intellectual. For the people who make up our human society, I opted to create the best product to foster dialogue, not to cause separation. Those who are seeking to use this as research will find the horizon line so clear between the god of Islam and the God of Christianity.

Notes

The English translation of the Qur'an does not accurately reflect the Arabic version of the original, especially when the verse is offensive to the feelings and beliefs of Westerners. The meaning of some verses of the Qur'an are changed in translation to make them appear softer, to deceive Westerners. For example, Qur'an 3:54 describes Allah as a great planner in the English translation, softening the true intended meaning, that Allah is the best of deceivers.

Translation of Bible verses used in this text are mostly New Living Translation (NLT), with some English Standard Version (ESV), and The New King James Version (NKJV).

Chapter I
Of the Origin & History

Islam appeared in Hijaz, the northwestern region of the Arabian Peninsula, with a particular focus on the cities of Mecca and Yathrib, which later combined by Islam and was called "Al-Madina."

Mecca was a small commercial center, and Yathrib had a thriving agricultural industry where most of the local Arabs were nomadic cattle herders. The tribe was the principal organization of Arabic social and political life, providing them with security and a sense of identity. Islam unites everything under the umbrella of religion, rejecting any secularism, leaving no separation between the mosque and the state in Islamic rule. Mohammed established and became leader of the first Islamic state in "Al-Madina."

There are five pillars of Islam. They are:

1. Islamic Declaration: "There is no god but Allah, and Mohammed is the messenger of Allah." Recitation of the testimony in the presence of a Muslim makes a person a Muslim. When a child is born, his father or grandfather whispers the declaration in his ear to make him a Muslim.

2. Liturgical five prayers a day requiring ablution, washing all exposed parts of the body with water, or sand, if water is not available (Surat Almaida 5:6). If the Muslim

touches the non-Muslim, he becomes defiled, and should perform ablutions again.

3. Zakat (obligatory charity).

4. The fasting month of Ramadan: During the whole month of Ramadan, every Muslim, fourteen years or older, must refrain from eating, drinking, smoking, and sexual intercourse from dawn to sunset. Not fasting without a legitimate excuse is a sin that is unforgivable (Baqarah 2:183-187). Islam follows the lunar calendar, which is shorter than the Western calendar by either ten or twelve days. Thus, the month of Ramadan occurs during different seasons of the year.

5. Pilgrimage to Mecca: Muslims who can afford to, must do it at least once in their lifetime. The main shrine of Islam is the Kaaba in the city of Mecca, which is off limits to non-Muslims. According to Islamic beliefs, Adam built the cube of the Kaaba, then Abraham and his son, Ishmael, finalized the purification of the site.

On the contrary, the Bible tells us that Abraham did not travel to the Arabian Peninsula. History tells us that the Kaaba was a pagan temple erected for the sanctity of all the Arab tribes. It was the house of idols in the time of Mohammed, who destroyed many pagan idols. Muslims traditionally pray in the direction of the Kaaba, and circumnavigate around it seven times in their pilgrimage. One corner of the Kaaba stone is venerated above the rest, a small black area, and likely part of a meteorite or an old statue of a pagan god.

Muslims believe that Mohammed is the prophet who

received the Qur'an, texts that frame the religion, from the god of Islam, beginning in 610 AD and ending before his death in 632 AD. The primary source for the teachings and beliefs of the Islamic religion and its practice is the Qur'an. Mohammed claimed that the Qur'an was a righteous miracle sent down from god, that it is the literal word of the "eternal, uncreated god of Islam." The Qur'an is the word of their god: he has spoken it and is speaking with it now and will speak on judgment day. These writings were believed to have been given to Mohammed by the angel Gabriel. Without any input or influence by Mohammed, that he was just the messenger, not its author. However, it is logical to conclude (Qur'an 3:3: He has sent down upon you, [O Muhammed], the Book in truth, confirming what was before it. And He revealed the Torah and the Gospel) that Islam's book may also include certain human thoughts, according to Mohammed's personality.

The Qur'an consists of 114 books (Sura), each with its own number and address. The Sura are arranged according to length, the longer at the beginning of the Qur'an, and the shortest Sura in the end. The only exception is Sura 1 (Fatiha), which contains seven verses. The arrangement is also organized in order to characterize them as "Makiya" or "Mediniya," pertaining to whether Mohammed had been given the verses before or after his emigration from Mecca to Medina in 622 AD. He was forced to move to save his life. Tribal leaders want to kill him because he was changing the structure of the tribal society in that time, and they were losing their authority. The Hadith is an additional set of writings complementary to the Qur'an, and is necessary to gain an understanding of the historical context and chronology of the Qur'an. It also contains historical information about the life, the works, and the sayings of Mohammed.

Theologians base their rules of Islamic law on four different sources: first, the Qur'an, second, the Hadith, third, Consensus (consensus among Muslim scholars on the issue), and fourth, Measurement (reasoning on the basis of similarity). According to Shiite scholars, theories are often solved by using individual reasoning of measurement.

The Qur'an declares that Mohammed came to renew the religion of Abraham (Nisa' 4:125). In fact, Islam is based on laws that require submission to the will of their god, enslaving Muslims by their fear of punishment, leaving no room for God's love and friendship. Therefore, contrary to this statement of the Qur'an, Islam contradicts and rejects the religion of Abraham. We know from the Bible that the original religion of Abraham did not include law, but the foundations of a covenant including a promise between God and Abraham. God established this covenant before giving the law to Moses 430 years later (Galatians 3:17). Abraham was not under the Law of Moses; instead his religion was based on his belief in the promise of God, "I will bless those who bless you, and curse those who curse you. All the nations of the earth will be blessed through you," Genesis 12:3. God fulfilled that promise in the birth of Jesus, the Messiah, through the descendants of Abraham. Abraham received God's love and promises because of his faith alone, which is why he is called a "friend of God" and not just a slave to Him.

When Mohammed died on June 8, 632 AD, his rule had encompassed the bulk of the Arabian Peninsula, and within 100 years of his death, Islamic armies established a vast Islamic empire stretching from Central Asia to the north of India, the Middle East, North Africa and Iberia. Initially, Islamic occupiers lived richly in cities like military garrisons, enjoying a lifestyle supported by new taxes on the occupied territories and the spoils of ongoing military campaigns.

About 85 percent of Muslims belong to Sunni Islam, and about 12 percent to Shia Islam. When using the term "Islam," it's referring to the religion or religious teaching. Muslims refer to people who believe and follow the religion of Islam, whether they practice Islam or not. The roots of the split between Sunnis and Shiites go back to the historical struggle to succeed Mohammed upon his death. A majority of Muslim leaders chose Abu Bakr, a close follower of Mohammed, to be the first Caliph, the title given to each leader of the Islamic rule after the reign of Mohammed. A small number of people wanted Ali ibn Abi Talib, Mohammed's cousin and husband of Mohammed's daughter, Fatima, to be his successor. Eventually, Ali was assassinated in 661 AD, but the Shiite movement sprung forward from the original supporters of Ali. According to Shiite belief, the leader, or imam, will be a Muslim descendant of Ali from his wife, Fatima, daughter of Mohammed. Shiites are awaiting the Twelfth Imam (referred to as the Imam Mahdi), and during this waiting period, they are given full authority over prominent Muslim legal and religious scholars.

Islam called Jews and Christians "People of the Book," "Ahil Althomah," or "protected peoples" in the occupied territories, and considered them inferior to Muslims. Jews and Christians were prevented from proselytizing their religion or their faith and from building any new places of worship. They were required to pay tribute, a tax imposed on non-Muslims only. In many places, and different areas, "Ahil Althomah" were required to wear distinctive clothing, and they were forbidden to carry arms. This persecution is one of the factors that forced many non-Muslims to convert to Islam.

Chapter II
Of the Nature of Allah, Mohammed, and Jesus

In the beginning and above all, we need to discuss the deity of Islam. To understand any religion from theological, philosophical, and moral matters, we must first understand the nature of the deity in that religion. When we understand the deity, we will understand the essence, the depth of legislation, and the culture of that belief.

Allah is an Arabic word that is derived from Canaanite roots, and was used in the Aramaic (Allahi) and Chaldean (Allaha) languages. The story of the name goes back to the Canaanites, who had many gods, one that was called Ealat. There is a substantial difference between Ealat and Allah; Ealat meaning ANY god, not a specific one and Allah meaning "god the creator" or "one god." The term Allah was developed during the pagan era of the Arabian Peninsula.

The ancient Arabic language is very emotional, relying on tones and origin of sounds to add to the meaning of each word. The name Allah, linguistically, contains a strong, heavy L. This exaggeration of the L, which becomes a double letter in Arabic, is another indication of the importance of the word, the deity implied. The adding of the letter Ha, bringing the word to Allah, is also very purposeful. They call Ha the unseen or invisible letter because the sound comes from deep within the chest, lending "unseen" as an attribute of the deity of Allah. These are metaphysical symbols meaning Allah, the one eternal, both present and also behind the scenes. Today, the term is widely used in both Arabic and Aramaic Bibles. The pagan era saw the worship of many gods at Mecca (modern Saudi Arabia). Most were created by man, crafted from wood, or stone, and some were even made from dates, which would then be eaten by the hungry worshiper. Most Muslims believed their religion was developed to eliminate their paganistic multiple gods, and were skeptical that it would bring proof of their monotheistic god, Allah, the god of Abraham and Jacob and Mohammed.

To prove the word Allah existed long before Mohammed, we should go back to the connotation. The emergence of the term was cultural. As a name, Allah existed in Arabic culture before Mohammed was reported to have received his revelation of god, and even before he was born. This is proven in that his father's name was Abdullah, meaning "servant of Allah." The word actually was not related at all to Islam, the religion. The Qur'an simply redefined the original word Allah, which had nothing to do with the divine personality presented by Mohammed in the Qur'an.

The Bible presents the truth of God in the person of His incarnate Son, Jesus Christ, the sole heir of the living God. "And the Word became flesh and dwelt among us and we beheld his glory, glory as of the only begotten from the Father, full of grace and truth," John 1:14; 14:6. The Christian faith is centered on Jesus Christ; His life, death and resurrection form the foundation of Christianity. Jesus Christ is the most important message, in that God has spectacularly revealed Himself, not only through the Bible, but also in the history of the human. Jesus willingly laid aside His deity in order to be born of the flesh, to relate to humans on their level of understanding. In Christ, the believer is born again and ennobled by Grace, becoming a joint heir with Him, to the kingdom of God. God cares about the affairs of humans and has had a tremendous effect on human history. Everything from God, and in God, was created for the Son, who was present from the beginning, "In the beginning the Word already existed. The Word was with God, and the Word was God," John 1:1 (NLT).

The Holy Spirit of the living God is the force at work in the Christian church, creating a desire for spiritual renewal and sanctification, which takes place internally, in order to gradually become more like Jesus Christ. Jesus told the disciples He would be leaving them, but that He would send "The Comforter" to fill them with the power to carry on in His absence, "But when the Father sends the Advocate as my representative—that is, the Holy Spirit—he will teach you everything and will remind you of everything I have told you," John 14:26 (NLT). Prior to Jesus' ascension into Heaven, the Holy Spirit had appeared in bodily forms, and His power would come upon people, enabling them to do great things in the name of God. After the day of Pentecost, however, the Holy Spirit began indwelling believers, becoming an internal witness, teacher, moral compass, and a guarantee of eternal salvation. "Humans can reproduce only human life, but the Holy Spirit gives birth to spiritual life," John 3:6 (NLT).

True Christian faith consists of three basic elements: first, the emotional component, the bond linking the love between God and the human; second, the intellectual surrendering of the state of mind, having the faith to accept Christian fundamentals, the basic doctrines of Christianity; and third, voluntary commitment to follow the teachings of Jesus Christ. Thus, true Christian faith includes the entire human: his mind, his passion, and his will. Christian life is based on love for the one true and living God and a love for others.

All the main denominations of the Christian religion share, to some degree, the treasure of Christ as the missing part of humankind (2 Corinthians 4:7). It is expected that the Christian faith, with nearly 2.2 billion followers, will have different doctrines, differences inherent to the fallen nature of mankind. It is important to not try to minimize the importance of these differences. However, it is imperative to emphasize the fact that all Christian denominations, including many conservative, Protestant denominations, believe in the same basic principles vital to the Christian faith. These include the divine inspiration of the Bible, the Holy Trinity, the divinity of Christ, the virgin birth of Christ, the miracles of Christ, Christ's crucifixion and resurrection, His second coming in glory and power, the work of the Holy Spirit, salvation, the resurrection of the dead, final judgment, etc. What unites the various Christian denominations is far greater than what divides them.

The Qur'an does not talk about the love of god to Mohammed, or the love of Mohammed to god; instead, Mohammed described himself as the servant of Allah (Our Servant Muhammad 2:23). There is unfortunately no reference to love as a description of Allah, in the 99 names of the Islamic god. In contrast, Jesus Christ's relationship with God the Father is based on mutual divine love. God the Father spoke of His love for His Son incarnate, "But even as he spoke, a bright cloud overshadowed them, and a voice from the cloud said, 'This is my dearly loved Son, who brings me great joy. Listen to him,'" Matthew 17:5; 12:18; 3:17. The obedience of Jesus Christ is evidence of His love for God the Father (John 14:31). Divine Love as the supreme example of love, is advocated by Jesus, "I have loved you even as the Father has loved me. Remain in my love. This is my commandment: Love each other in the same way I have loved you. There is no greater love than to lay down one's life for one's friends," John 15:9, 12-13; 3:16.

Although the Qur'an offers a passing reference to the love of Islam's god in verse 11:90, it focuses more on obedience to the god of Islam as a slave to his master (Qur'an 50:8), (Qur'an

8:13). Mohammed imposed brutal punishments, claiming that God willed them, to keep the followers faithful: removing the skin, cutting body parts off, or stoning to death, etc. In addition, the god of Islam shows a deep dislike of any disbelievers (Qur'an 3:32). His goal is to use deception in order to fill the hell he created (Qur'an 32:13).

Christian teachings contradict Islamic teachings. The eternal Divine love between God the Father and Jesus Christ, the incarnate Son, is also shared in their relationship with humanity. Jesus said to His disciples that God the Father loves them, "...for the Father himself loves you dearly because you love me and believe that I came from God," John 16:27. Christ also expressed His love to His followers, "I have loved you even as the Father has loved me. Remain in my love. When you obey my commandments, you remain in my love, just as I obey my Father's commandments and remain in His love," John 15:9-10. In fact, He loved them so much that He sacrificed His life on earth to save them from eternal damnation (John 10:14-15). He raised His faithful disciples to the level of friends, "I no longer call you slaves, because a master doesn't confide in his slaves. Now you are my friends, since I have told you everything the Father told me," John 15:15.

In addition to His love for His followers, Jesus loved those who did not believe in Him and tried to help them, "When Jesus heard this, he told them, 'Healthy people don't need a doctor—sick people do. I have come to call not those who think they are righteous, but those who know they are sinners,'" Mark 2:17; John 4:7-26; Luke 7:36-50; 15:1-2; 23:39-43. Christ was modeling this attribute of God the Father, who instructs us to also emulate this, "Love your enemies! Do good to them. Lend to them without expecting to be repaid. Then your reward from heaven will be very great, and you will truly be acting as children of the Most High, for he is kind to those who are unthankful and wicked. You must be compassionate, just as your Father is compassionate," Luke 6:35-36; Matthew 5:45; John 3:16-17; Romans 5:8.

Chapter III
Of the Fundamentals

In examining any belief, we should look for its clarity, because complicated, abstract ideas are harder to follow. Islam claims that it is clearly summarized, that there is one creator of this entire fascinating universe. The monotheistic view portrayed is that there are no partnerships, no wife and no son. This claim of clarity matches the human mind because the mind demands a linking structure between ideas, uniting them in a single cause. This area of doctrine is indeed clear, but it seems illogical that Islam then demands blind followers, and doesn't allow for debate, as it says in the Qur'an, verse 59:7, "And whatever the Messenger has given you—take; and what he has forbidden you—refrain from. And fear Allah; indeed, Allah is severe in punishment."

The term Islam means submission, without question. Because faith usually is beyond the mind's ability to rationalize, only becoming understood with wisdom, I always say, he who experiences what I have would know what I know.

On the other hand, Islam claims to be of a pure nature, not foreign or contradictory to the true human nature, fully in sync, in perfect harmony with each other. According to the Islamic teaching's perspective, a small child, untouched and unaffected by parents or society, will naturally grow up believing in Islam. Every child is born in Islamic nature but the parents and surroundings can make him a Jew or Christian, as it says in the Qur'an, verse 30:30: "So direct your face toward the religion, inclining to truth. The fitrah [pure nature] of Allah upon which He has created all people, no change should there be in the creation of Allah. That is the correct religion, but most of the people do not know."

Islam is a theoretical belief. Apologetically, it is not proven and has no basis in historical evidence. It is just an argument. It obligates its followers to blindly accept Mohammed's writings, and not respect the mind's underlying desire to question religious thought, unless by the evidence in the Qur'an or Sun'aa (Mohammed's sayings). Indeed, the followers are forbidden to go deeper and examine the teachings for themselves.

"And do not pursue that of which you have no knowledge. Indeed, the hearing, the sight and the heart—about all those [one] will be questioned," Qur'an 17:36.

In fact, those who oppose or question Mohammed's writings, according to the principle of Islam, bear the entire burden of proof when prompting debate.

"And they say, 'None will enter Paradise except one who is a Jew or a Christian.' That is merely their wishful thinking, Say, 'Produce your proof, if you should be truthful,'" Qur'an 2:111.

The principle of Islam in the Qur'an is changeable, because it is not based on evidence or proof. We see the discourse of the Qur'an sometimes say, "No change is there in the words of Allah. That is what is the great attainment," in verse 10:64 of the Qur'an, because Allah guaranteed to keep his word, to not fail or not to change, as it says in the Qur'an, verse 15:9, "Indeed, it is We who sent down the Qur'an and indeed, We will be its guardian." Also, Allah says: "We do not abrogate a verse or cause it to be forgotten except that We bring forth [one] better than it or similar to it. Do you not know that Allah is over all things competent?" in the Qur'an, verse 2:106.

"Allah eliminates what He wills or confirms, and with Him

is the Mother of the Book," Qur'an 13:39.

"And when We substitute a verse in place of a verse—and Allah is most knowing of what He sends down—they say, 'You, O Muhammad, are but an inventor of lies.' But most of them do not know," Qur'an 16:101.

This is an inconsistent principle. It is non-stationary, allowing for increase and decrease, and is open to distortion. In fact, it seems like Allah changes his mind according to circumstances that are out of his control.

Islam keeps its deity above description, indescribable, as it says in the Qur'an, verse 42:11, "There is nothing like unto Him, and He is the Hearing, the seeing."

"Nor is there to Him any equivalent," Qur'an 112:4.

"Do you know of any similarity to Him?" Qur'an 19:65.

Islamic faith is a combination of blind submission, mimicry of belief and exaggeration to penetrate the mind's ability to understand and grasp the qualities of god, as it says in the Qur'an, verse 20:110, "Allah knows what is presently before them and what will be after them, but they do not encompass it in knowledge."

According to Islamic law, the Muslim should lie in some cases, as it says in the Qur'an, verse 2:225, "Allah does not impose blame upon you for what is unintentional in your oaths," despite the fact that the Qur'an does not allow Muslims to deceive each other. Islam encourages lying in giving directions to someone who intends to do something wrong, in the settlement of disputes in war, in domestic disputes, and to gain advantages over non-Muslims.

Dissimulation is the act of lying, especially to non-Muslims, in order to promote, protect or preserve Islam, as it says in the Qur'an, verse 3:28, "Let not believers take disbelievers as allies rather than believers. And whoever [of you] does that has nothing with Allah, except when taking precaution against them in prudence. And Allah warns you of Himself, and to Allah is the [final] destination."

"Whoever disbelieves in Allah after his belief...except for one who is forced [to renounce his religion] while his heart is secure in faith. But those who [willingly] open their breasts to disbelief, upon them is wrath from Allah, and for them is a great punishment," Qur'an 16:106.

Islam also encourages followers to lie as a means to hide the true faith in some circumstances. Friendship between Muslims and non-Muslims may appear genuine, but it is only external. A Muslim may be smiling in the face of a non-Muslim, but will curse them in his heart. Dissimulation leads to double, deceptive messages, the one for Muslims being quite different from what is portrayed to the non-Muslims. In Islam there are two ethical standards: one to deal with Muslims and another to deal with non-Muslims. In fact, the Qur'an even describes the Muslim god as "the best of deceivers," as it says in verse 3:52, "And the disbelievers deceive, but Allah deceives too. And Allah is the best of deceivers."

"Indeed, the hypocrites think to deceive Allah, but He is deceiving them," Qur'an 4:142.

"Allah is swifter in cunning," Qur'an 10:21.

Therefore, the principle of dissimulation is consistent with the character of Allah making lying and deception an integral part of tradition and the Islamic way of life.

Islam permits a Muslim to lie under oath in good conscience, as long as he thinks he is doing so for the progress of Islam, as Qur'an 5:89 states, "Allah will not impose blame upon you for what is meaningless in your oaths, but He will impose blame upon you for breaking what you intended of oaths. So its expiation is the feeding of ten needy people from the average of that which you feed your own families or clothing them or the freeing of a slave. But whoever cannot find or afford it—then a fast of three days is required. That is the expiation for oaths when you have sworn. But guard your oaths. Thus does Allah make clear to you His verses that you may be grateful."

Islamic groups and governments use peace talks and ceasefire agreements to buy time so they can put together new plans, regroup and prepare themselves to achieve a military victory. They will break their agreements when they reach a point of strength.

Islamists benefit from the principle of dissimulation in the defense of Islam. In fact, the English translation of the Qur'an does not accurately reflect the Arabic version of the original, especially when the verse is offensive to the feelings and beliefs of Westerners. The meaning of some verses of the Qur'an are changed in translation to make them appear softer, to deceive Westerners. They cite (Mecca verses) from the Qur'an calling for peace and tolerance toward non-Muslims. This is a significant distortion of Islam, because Muslims know full well that these verses were calls to violence against non-Muslims, but were abrogated by civilians concerned about seeming intolerant. These tactics are used to outwit people who do not see the realities of Islam and Sharia.

In contrast, through millions of testimonies of Christians, they don't deny their faith in Jesus Christ under persecution, even if it leads to martyrdom. Jesus said, "But whoever denies me before men, I also will deny before my Father who is in heaven," Matthew 10:33; Mark 8:38; Luke 9:26, 12:9. "If we endure, we will also reign with him; if we deny him, he also will deny us," 2 Timothy 2:12. In addition, the God of the Bible condemns lying, encourages honesty: "Do not steal. Do not deceive or cheat one another. Do not bring shame on the name of your God by using it to swear falsely. I am the Lord," Leviticus 19:11-12, and prohibits perjury: "You must not testify falsely against your neighbor," Exodus 20:16.

Many Muslims believe that the Gospel of Jesus Christ was only for the children of Israel, as noted in the Qur'an, verses 5:46-47. They attribute the spread of Christianity in the world to the teachings of the Church to the First Nations. In fact, after His resurrection from the dead, Christ's disciples went out to preach Christianity to ALL the nations of the earth: "And Jesus came and spoke unto them, saying, 'I have been given all authority in heaven and on earth. Go therefore and make disciples of all nations, baptizing them in the name of the Father and of the Son and of the Holy Spirit,'" Matthew 28:18-19; Acts 1:8 (NLT).

The main message of Christianity is that Jesus Christ is the Word (Son) of God, incarnate and that He died on the cross, was buried and rose from the dead three days later. It is completely contrary to the central message of Islam, which is that He is not the eternal Son of God, Jesus did not die on the cross, did not rise from the dead after three days, and that there is no need to declare prophets of any new religions after Christ, for the following reasons:

1. Jesus Christ is the Word (Son) of God incarnate. Christ is the final revelation of God, by whom all prophecies proclaiming His coming have been fulfilled and all the revelation is complete. On the other hand, still expected in the future of Christianity, is the revelation of the false prophet and the Antichrist (2 Thessalonians 3; Revelation 19:20; 20:10), prior to the second coming of Christ in His full glory, to judge the living and the dead at the end of this era.

2. After His ascension into heaven, Christ sent the Holy Spirit of the living God in His place to continue teaching

the faithful and guiding His Church on earth. The Holy Spirit instructs believers on their journey in Christ, and guides them in the faith and their gradual growth toward a holy life. God says, "...I will pour out my Spirit upon all people. Your sons and daughters will prophesy. Your old men will dream dreams, and your young men will see visions. In those days I will pour out my Spirit even on servants—men and women alike," Acts 2:17-18; Joel 2:28-29 (NLT). "Clearly, you are a letter from Christ showing the result of our ministry among you. This 'letter' is written not with pen and ink, but with the Spirit of the living God. It is carved not on tablets of stone, but on human hearts," 2 Corinthians 3:3 (NLT). Therefore, there is no need for further prophets to establish a new religion after Jesus, as the Spirit of the Living God dwells within us, completing the work begun by Jesus (Matthew 21:33-44).

3. One of the main reasons for sending prophets is that God wants to improve the ethics of humans, as they are in a constant motion and evolution toward moral maturity. Every major prophet takes the morality of humans to a higher degree. For example, God gave Moses a law saying, "But if there is further injury, the punishment must match the injury: a life for a life, an eye for an eye, a tooth for a tooth, a hand for a hand, a foot for a foot," Exodus 21:23-25 (NLT). The ancient custom before the time of Moses was that the punishment should be greater than the original offense. The Law of Moses commuted that previous sentencing in order to prevent the occurrence of deadly violence that could spiral out of control. Rather than exacting revenge ten times greater,

there would be equality in the suffering. This was a development of human morality to a much higher level.

Jesus came after Moses by about fourteen centuries, and raised humanity to the level of moral ideal, calling for love and forgiveness rather than revenge. "You have heard that it was said, an eye for an eye, tooth for tooth. But I say to you, Love your enemies, bless them that curse you. Do good to those who hate you and pray for those who mistreat you and persecute you, that you may be sons of your Father who is in heaven. It is his son who shines on the righteous and the wicked, and sends rain on the righteous and the unrighteous," Matthew 5:38, 44-45. "Dear friends, never take revenge. Leave that to the righteous anger of God. For the Scriptures say, 'I will take revenge; I will pay them back,' says the Lord. Instead, 'If your enemies are hungry, feed them. If they are thirsty, give them something to drink. In doing this, you will heap burning coals of shame on their heads,'" Romans 12:19-21 (NLT). Indeed, Jesus applied this teaching, personally, in His life on earth to give the highest example of love and forgiveness. While He was bleeding and suffering from the pain of death on the cross, He did not condemn those who crucified Him and did not curse them with death and destruction. Instead, He prayed for forgiveness for them, "When they came to a place called The Skull, they nailed him to the cross. And the criminals were also crucified—one on his right and one on his left. Jesus said, Father, forgive them, for they don't know what they are doing." Luke 23:33-34 (NLT).

Unlike the strong, moral character of forgiveness and tolerance modeled by Jesus, the teachings of Islam are a huge step backwards in the ethics of human beings. Islam calls for killing and intolerance, as the Qur'an, verse 2:178 says, "O you who have believed, prescribed for you is legal retribution for those murdered—the free for the free, the slave for the slave, and the female for the female. But whoever overlooks from his brother anything, and then there should be a suitable follow-up and payment to him with good conduct. This is alleviation from your Lord and a mercy. But whoever transgresses after that will have a painful punishment."

Islam permits, and even encourages, polygamy and the taking of concubines, whereas monogamy is God's design in the Bible. Mohammed took for himself Mary of Egypt (she was Christian), who was not among his wives, but of his concubines. He also practiced and permitted incestuous marriage, Mohammed married a daughter of his adopted son Zaid, Zainab, as noted in the Qur'an, verse 33:37: "And [remember, O Muhammad], when you said to the one on whom Allah bestowed favor and you bestowed favor, 'Keep your wife and fear Allah,' while you concealed within yourself that which Allah is to disclose. And you feared the people, while Allah has more right that you fear Him. So when Zayd had no longer any need for her, We married her to you in order that there not be upon the believers any discomfort concerning the wives of their adopted sons when they no longer have need of them. And ever is the command of Allah accomplished"; and wife-beating, "So righteous women are devoutly obedient, guarding in [the husband's] absence what Allah would have them guard. But those [wives] from whom you fear arrogance—[first] advise them; [then if they persist], forsake them in bed; and [finally], strike them. But if they obey you [once more], seek no means against them. Indeed, Allah is ever Exalted and Grand," Qur'an 4:34.

Moses and Jesus did not condone this kind of moral degradation. One of the most important teachings central to Christianity is the love of God and love for each other. "For God loved the world so much that he gave his one and only Son, so that everyone who believes in him will not perish but have eternal life," John 3:16. "But anyone who does not love, does not know God, for God is love," 1 John 4:8. Jesus commanded Christians to love God and their neighbors. "Jesus replied, 'You must love the Lord your God with all your heart, all your soul, and all your mind.' This is the first and greatest commandment. A second is equally important: 'Love your neighbor as yourself.' The entire law and all the demands of the prophets are based on these two commandments," Matthew 22:37-40; Mark 12:28-31; John 13:34-35; 15:9, 12; Romans 13:10; 1 John 4:7-10, 15-16, 20-21; 1 Peter 3:8-9.

In His teachings and miracles, Jesus focused on two of the most important facts: the love of God is far superior to that of humans, and humans can accept this love and allow it to flow through them to others. Love manifests itself in relationships. God's love should cause a desire to submit totally to Him, and live every day to His satisfaction. This is the highest level of worship that we can give to God.

Christianity teaches that forgiveness is the treatment for the broken relationship between Christ and the sinner who repents. There is only one way to forgiveness and reconciliation with God: to accept the atonement provided by Christ on the cross for the faithful, repentant sinner. "But God demonstrates His own love for us in that while we were yet sinners, Christ died for us," Romans 5:8; 1 Peter 3:18. Without Christ's death, there would be no hope for the sinner, but he who puts his faith in Christ has complete forgiveness for his fallen, sinful nature through Christ's suffering. "But he was pierced for our transgressions; he was crushed for our iniquities; upon him was the chastisement that brought us peace, and with his wounds we are healed," Isaiah 53:5 (ESV).

God gives the Gospel of grace to all those who believe in Jesus Christ as their Lord and Savior. All that is required is that they accept the free gift of atonement provided by Christ on the cross. "...But if anyone does sin, we have an advocate with the Father, Jesus Christ the righteous. He is the propitiation for our sins, and not for ours only but also for the sins of the whole world," 1 John 2:1-2; Romans 5:1-2; 1 Peter 2:24-25; Ephesians 1:7-8. "How much more will the blood of Christ, who through the eternal Spirit offered himself without blemish to God, purify our conscience from dead works to serve the living God," Hebrews 9:14; "And there is salvation in no one else, for there is no other name under heaven given among men by which we must be saved," Acts 4:12. This forgiveness of the repentant believer frees Christians from the bondage of sin and spiritual death (Romans 6:6-7; Galatians 5:13; 1 Peter 2:16). Christians are instructed to forgive others to expand the scope of the forgiveness they have received from God.

Islam does not offer any means for forgiveness of sins by the Muslim god or by Islamic law. There is no middleman for the Muslim, pleading with his or her god for forgiveness. Muslims have no guarantee that their sins are forgiven them after repentance, as it says in verse 9:102 of the Qur'an, "And [there are] others who have acknowledged their sins. They had mixed a righteous deed with another that was bad."

"And if Allah were to impose blame on the people for their wrongdoing, He would not have left upon the earth any creature, but He defers them for a specified term. And when their term has come, they will not remain behind an hour, nor will they precede it," Qur'an 16: 61.

Islam's god gives grace randomly to those who wish for it, Qur'an 5:18, "They have certainly disbelieved who say that Allah is Christ, the son of Mary. Say, Then who could prevent

Allah at all if He had intended to destroy Christ, the son of Mary, or his mother or everyone on the earth?"

In fact, no Muslim can be assured forgiveness because the Islamic god, himself, is a master of deception and evil, and he calls his followers to sin and evil. "But those who deny our verses are deaf and dumb within darknesses. Whomever Allah wills—He leaves astray; and whomever He wills—He puts him on a straight path," Qur'an 6:39.

"Allah sends astray thereby whom He wills and guides whom He wills. And He is the Exalted in Might, the Wise," Qur'an 14:4. Islam teaches that forgiveness of sins only occurs in eternity.

The Qur'an tells that the god of Islam created Adam and breathed into his soul, as it says in verse 32:9, "Then He proportioned him and breathed into him from His created soul." It does not mention anything about the creation of Eve, when it occurred or how. Islam believes that man does not resemble God in every way, and it is understood that God breathing into the spirit of Adam was meant to impart knowledge and the abilities of the human will.

The Bible tells that God created Adam from the dust of the earth, then created Eve from one of Adam's ribs (Genesis 1:26-27; 2: 7, 18-23), making her equal to Adam. God created man in his own image, which refers first to the rights to inheritance and nobility, and also to the capacity of man to develop and grow similar to God in terms of moral perfection and holiness.

Islam teaches that obedience to its god is the way to salvation. This includes good works, a true faith in their god, his books, his messenger, and the day of judgment. It is also imperative to practice the five pillars of the Islamic ritual of worship. Islamic salvation does not lead to liberation from the grip of sin on the mind, the heart, and the life of the believer in the present era, nor does it lead to a spiritual renewal. Islam believes all humanity is basically good, not born in a naturally sinful nature, like the Bible teaches.

The Qur'an describes Islam's god as merciful and just at the same time. Unfortunately, Islam does not offer a way to satisfy the demands of their god's judgment and wrath against sin in order to allow mercy and forgiveness to flow toward sinners. As mentioned above, forgiveness in Islam happens randomly, haphazardly, without any basis. Islam does not provide a path to redemption and salvation, like the sacrifice made by Jesus on the cross to satisfy the justice of God. Based on this sacrifice, God can justify the penitents who accept the atonement provided by Christ for them. Jesus has taken the penalty for their sins and paid the price on their behalf, by dying on the cross.

The Bible teaches that sin committed by any human is against an infinite God, and therefore should be punishable by death. Good works and obedience to God are also requirements of a Christian life, but even a nice man would not be a sufficient atonement to God. It is not enough to pay for the sins of man (Romans 3:10). Therefore, the idea of the balance of the judgment, weighing the good deeds of a person against his evil deeds, presents the wrong idea. God's judgment is supreme, and He alone decides where each human soul will spend eternity. Good deeds do not cover or compensate for evil, just as they do not remove the guilt of bad deeds. Good works are mixed in with bad acts in every person's life, like an omelet that contains good eggs and rotten eggs. No one would eat it. We would also not accept a glass of water if a drop of ink has been added to it. Good efforts do not erase bad deeds, not in human laws, nor in the laws of God. No man can cancel the sins committed in the past.

Law decides what is right and what is wrong, but the law

cannot change and purify the person internally and make him valid. It is simply the standard that is used to judge a person. God cannot accept a real life, which is contaminated by sin, as holy. Good deeds do not cure the person from the disease of sin, nor will they lead to internal change, cleansing and lifting the curse of a fallen human nature (Galatians 5:4). Keeping the law, in itself, does not bridge the great divide that separates fallen humanity from the Holy God. Therefore, one can never do enough good deeds to satisfy the rift between God and man. "I do not nullify the grace of God, for if righteousness were through the law, then Christ died for no purpose," Galatians 2:21. "We have all become like one who is unclean, and all our righteous deeds are like a polluted garment. We all fade like a leaf, and our iniquities, like the wind, take us away," Isaiah 64:6. "Yet we know that a person is not justified by works of the law but through faith in Jesus Christ, so we also have believed in Christ Jesus, in order to be justified by faith in Christ and not by works of the law, because by works of the law no one will be justified," Galatians 2:16. "For whoever keeps the whole law but fails in one point has become accountable for all of it," James 2:10. If the sinner repents and accepts the atonement of Jesus Christ, his faith is real and the account of his sin is charged to Christ, who took the punishment on the cross.

If it was possible to renew human nature through direction and guidance only, why did God send many messengers over the centuries, instead of just one prophet? Why did humans continue in their disobedience and unrighteousness? After the fall of Adam and Eve, it was obvious mankind could not be saved with direction and guidance only. It showed that human nature cannot be renewed and that an uncorrupted solution needed to be provided. A lost humanity needs redemption, not just a revelation. This is the Christian plan of salvation by faith for the repentant believer who accepts the free gift of atonement provided by Christ on the cross. Islam does not provide a cure for the disease of sin, either. Neither does it provide a way to change the fallen human nature and sanctify the character of the person. Only Christ can change the person inside and give him a new nature.

Some Islamists objected to the crucifixion of Christ, denying it happened, believing that God would not allow His servant to suffer. This is the logic of human thought, not the mind of the Lord God. God declared through the prophet Isaiah, saying, "For my thoughts are not your thoughts, neither are your ways my ways, says the Lord," verse 55:8. Persecution suffered by many of the prophets of God proves the Qur'an's objection is not true, because many of the prophets and apostles have even been killed for their beliefs. Jesus triumphed over His enemies when God raised Him from the dead on the third day, claiming victory over sin, the devil and death. "...He foresaw and spoke about the resurrection of the Christ, that he was not abandoned to Hades, nor did his flesh see corruption. This Jesus God raised up, and of that we all are witnesses. Being therefore exalted at the right hand of God, and having received from the Father the promise of the Holy Spirit, he has poured out this that you yourselves are seeing and hearing," Acts 2: 31-33. "When the perishable puts on the imperishable, and the mortal puts on immortality, then shall come to pass the saying that is written, "Death is swallowed up in victory," 1 Corinthians 15:54. There is substantial historical proof of the resurrection of Jesus Christ from the dead, and God has accepted this sacrifice. This acceptance of the death and resurrection of Jesus Christ is evidence of God's mercy and justice toward a fallen humanity, "But God demonstrates His own love for us in that while we were yet sinners, Christ died for us," Romans 5:8. Christ said, "No one has greater love than this, than to lay down one's life for his friends," John 15:13 (NKJV). The Cross of Christ demonstrates God's love for the sinner as well as His hatred of sin. The reflection of the greatness of God in His love is uniquely superior to mankind through the Passion of Christ.

There is no principle in Islam of love and sacrifice. Islam teaches that a Muslim who commits a great sin (worships another god, denies the basic tenets of Islam, insults Mohammed, kills Muslims etc.), may be forgiven, or not, when repentant to the Islamic god. His forgiveness is granted at random, as in verse 5:18 of the Qur'an, "But the Jews and the Christians say, 'We are the children of Allah and His beloved.' Say, 'Then why does He punish you for your sins?' Rather, you are human beings from among those He has created. He forgives whom He wills, and He punishes whom He wills." It is hoped that the repentant sinner gets recognition and redemption, and that his work is acceptable: "Say, O Muhammad, "If you should love Allah, then follow me, so Allah will love you and forgive you your sins. And Allah is Forgiving and Merciful," Qur'an 3:31.

The only hope a Muslim has is that his deeds outweigh the balance of his transgressions, and the judgment is in his favor. As we have discussed previously, good works do not eliminate the sin, but later in his preaching, when Mohammed began sending military campaigns, he claimed that he had received a guaranteed way to earn the forgiveness of the Lord, the believers' consent to fight and die in the act of Islamic Jihad, as the Qur'an, verse 3:195, says, "And their Lord responded to them, 'Never will I allow to be lost the work of [any] worker among you, whether male or female; you are of one another. So those who emigrated or were evicted from their homes or were harmed in My cause or fought or were killed—I will surely remove from them their misdeeds, and I will surely admit them to gardens beneath which rivers flow as reward from Allah, and Allah has with Him the best reward.'" It is believed that a Muslim who dies in the act of Islamic Jihad goes directly to the Islamic paradise from his grave without waiting for the Day of Judgment. A Jihadist, any Muslim who kills others for the cause of Islam, bypasses any necessity for good works, and is immediately rewarded without judgment.

There is no guarantee of salvation in Islam for Muslims who do not participate in Islamic Jihad. Mohammed, himself, relied on his works and the mercy of his god to gain paradise. Because the Islamic god sends people to hell randomly, and is fickle in granting forgiveness, he cannot be trusted, so even Mohammed was worried about his eternal destiny and expressed skepticism and concern about whether his god would accept him: "Say, "I am not something original among the messengers, nor do I know what will be done with me or with you," Qur'an 46:9.

In fact, Mohammed asked Muslims to pray for his salvation in eternity: "Indeed, Allah and his angels confers prayer upon the Prophet. O you, who have believed, ask Allah to confer blessing upon him (Mohammed) and ask Allah to grant him peace," Qur'an 43:56. In the five daily Muslim prayers, one of the concluding prayers often says, "O Allah! Mercy on Mohammed and his descendants." If Mohammed is in peace in paradise, why would there be need to pray? There is no tranquility for Muslims. If the prophet of Islam was worried about his own salvation and eternal destiny, how must the average Muslim feel?

In contrast, the Bible gives assurances that all true believers, including the prophets and messengers of the real God, will go to heaven, in the presence of God, immediately after their deaths (2 Corinthians 5:1-10; Philippians 1:21, 23; 2 Timothy 4:6-8; Hebrews 12:22-24; Revelation 6:9-11; 7:9-17).

Islam declares that their god is the origin and source of good and evil alike. The discussion of absolute predestination brings up the subject of the Islamic god's absolute governance, and his attitude toward sinners. The Islamic god wants to lead people astray, as one of his goals is to fill hell with the souls of men. There is a vast difference in God's relationship with sinners and in the doctrine of Christianity on this important subject of judgment and eternal destiny.

According to the Islamic doctrine "torment of the grave," it is believed that the spirit of the Muslim returns to his body after being buried in the tomb and is fully aware of the feelings of being physically dead. Their spirits are then granted either paradise or torment of the grave, where torment angels smash the body with a huge iron hammer until it is turned to dust. The Islamic god then reassembles the body to again destroy it. He collapses the grave on the body, shattering the bones. A snake then enters the grave to feed on the corpse, but then the body regenerates to be eaten repeatedly. Mohammed declared that one of the greatest sins that cause the torment of the grave is not cleaning oneself after urinating. The only sure way to avoid the torment of the grave is martyrdom in Islamic Jihad.

The Islamic religion does not address what happens to the body destroyed by fire or devoured by animals, on land or in the sea. Physical evidence proves that the "torment of the grave" is just a fantasy and illusion because corpses, which were unearthed from their tombs, were found intact. Their bones were not broken and crushed, and the size of the tomb did not change.

Islam believes that Jesus returns to the earth in the end of time to judge the living and the dead and that every Muslim, evil or favored, first goes to hell after death (Qur'an 19:70-72). This means the Road to Islamic Paradise first passes through doors of hell.

In the description of the final judgment, Islam offers two

forms, the balance or the bridge.

1. The doctrine of the scales is the weighing of the good deeds of the Muslim against his evil deeds. Those whose good deeds exceed the bad will go on to paradise. Others will spend eternity in hell, as it says in the Qur'an, verses 7:8-9, "And the weighing [of deeds] that Day will be the truth. So those whose scales are heavy—it is they who will be the successful. And those whose scales are light—they are the ones who will lose themselves for what injustice they were doing toward Our verses."

What happens if the good works are equal to the bad? Islam does not answer this question. The god of Islam did not give clear instructions concerning the evaluation system and the weight of good deeds and bad.

The concept of the scales of judgment is not possible because good works, without salvation, is an external effort and does not lead to internal transformation and purification of the fallen human nature. The religious practices of Islam focus on the empty ritual of the superficial, and do not affect the status of the inner spiritual person. Good deeds cannot cover or cancel out sin, just as you cannot remove the guilt of the killer because he has done many good things in his life. Doing good deeds, in itself, is not able to bridge the vast gulf that separates the fallen human from the Holy God. Thus, good deeds cannot establish a fellowship between man and God. "We are all infected and impure with sin. When we display our righteous deeds, they are nothing but filthy rags. Like autumn leaves, we wither and fall, and our sins sweep us away like the wind," Isaiah 64:6. "I do not nullify the grace of God, for if righteousness were through the law, then Christ died for no purpose," Galatians 2:21.

2. The idea of the straight, narrow bridge is found in the Qur'an,

verses 7:23-24 and 36:66. In this last stage of the judgment, all Muslims must, in the end, arrive at this bridge across hell. Those who are righteous will go through quickly and safely, like the blowing of the wind, but those who have not reached a level acceptable to the god of Islam will fall into the flames of hell beneath them. This idea stems from Persian origins (Zoradocism).

The Qur'an refers to sexual behavior as immoral, yet their paradise promises indulgence in sensuality, sexual excess, and consumption of alcohol, in verse 47:15, "Is the description of Paradise, which the righteous are promised, wherein are rivers of water unaltered, rivers of milk the taste of which never changes, rivers of wine delicious to those who drink, and rivers of purified honey, in which they will have from all kinds of fruits and forgiveness from their Lord, like that of those who abide eternally in the Fire and are given to drink scalding water that will sever their intestines."

It is interesting to note that the things Islamists criticize and say are diabolical sins of the West are the basis of the Islamic paradise. This paradise is a reward only for the men. Muslim women are ignored completely, oppressed even, in the Islamic paradise. They do not have any assurances of receiving even one man. Again, women are only exploited to satisfy the men. The purpose of the existence of virgins in Islamic paradise is only to satisfy the sexual desires of Muslim men (Qur'an 2:25; also 37:39-49; 44:51-59; 47:15; 52:17-24; 56:12-39; 55:54-59 0.70-77; 78:31-34). Mohammed claimed that every Muslim would be given so many nymphs and the sexual ability equal to a hundred men when he enters the Islamic paradise. It seems like that there is a market for sex in paradise, which makes it look like a brothel. It is not a place of freedom and spirituality; instead they live in the bondage of greed for food, drink, sex, and lust.

Christ taught, "I tell you the truth, everyone who sins is a slave of sin. A slave is not a permanent member of the family, but a son is part of the family forever. So if the Son sets you free, you are truly free," John 8: 34-36 (NLT).

The Bible teaches that the human spirit is immortal by the grace of God (Matthew 22:32; Luke 20:38), and physical death occurs when the spirit leaves the body (2 Corinthians 5:1-4; 2 Peter 1:14; Philippians 1:23; 2 Timothy 4:6). The Bible distinguishes between two situations of the human soul after death: the condition directly after death, and the condition after the Judgment. Immediately following death, the spirit is either in spiritual bliss with the angels and saints who move in the presence of Jesus Christ (Luke 23:43; 16: 22-23), or in torment and darkness, separated from God. At this point, the fate of the person who died is eternal and cannot be changed (Luke 16: 19-31). However, a person does not receive reward or eternal punishment in full until after the resurrection and the final judgment.

There are different levels of rewards and punishments according to the fruits and works of each person prior to his death. Those who have died in Christ will be granted new, luminous, spiritual bodies that are not prone to corruption and death: "Then the righteous shine like the sun in the kingdom of their Father..." Matthew 13:43; 1 Corinthians 15:35-50; Philippians 3:20-21; 1 John 3:1-3, and will live in eternal, spiritual bliss in a new heaven (Revelation 21:1-4; 2 Peter 3:13). "...No eye has seen nor ear heard nor the heart of man imagined what God has prepared for those who love him," 1 Corinthians 2:9 (ESV). They will dwell in a state of reverence, in the company of the living God, in His eternal kingdom (Daniel 2:44, 7:13-14; 1 Thessalonians 4:17). There will be continuous growth toward the spiritual, infinite God, forever. Eternal bliss is spiritual bliss in the divine presence at the highest level of existence. It consists of salvation from pain, grief, corruption, etc., and will allow believers to finally see God in His majesty and glory, and have fellowship with the other souls of the righteous. It will not be a physical, voluptuous body, focused on greed, food, polygamy, and sensual pleasures. God of the Bible condemns and abhors this hyperbole and excess, "because the kingdom of God is not meat and drink but righteousness and peace and joy in the Holy Spirit," Romans 14:17; Habakkuk 1:13.

Christ taught that there is no human marriage in Heaven, "For in the resurrection they neither marry nor are married, but are as the angels of God in heaven," Matthew 22:30; Luke 20:35-36. This means that there is no physical intimacy in eternity.

Hell is a state of eternal torment for the wicked and the demons. Symbolically, it is represented by fire and worms that never die (Mark 9:43-48; 2 Thessalonians 1:8; Revelation 21:8), and where there will be weeping and gnashing of teeth (Matthew 8:12). This eternal Hell is called the lake of fire (Revelation 19:20) and also the second death (Revelation 20:14). The harshest of these eternal punishments is the deprivation of the glory of God and His eternal kingdom and everlasting separation from God, being cast into the outer darkness. Only in God, the Creator, can comfort be found.

Chapter IV
Of the Social Life & Cultural

Islam divides humanity into two layers: a top layer of Muslims (Qur'an 3:110), (Qur'an 9:33), and a layer of menial secularists and non-Muslims. The Qur'an strips non-Muslims of their humanity, and Mohammed despised them, calling them "evil beasts" (Qur'an 8:55), and "the evil of the wilderness" (Qur'an 98:6), (Qur'an 58:20). He claimed that the Jews had turned into monkeys (Qur'an 2:65), (Qur'an 7:166), and that Jews and Christians turned into pigs (Qur'an 5:59-60). He also said Jews look like donkeys (Qur'an 62:5), and that the Jews are cursed because of their unbelief (Qur'an 5:78). In addition, Mohammed declared that Muslims would annihilate the Jews at the end of the world (Bukhari, Jihad.)

According to the Qur'an, Muslims should avoid friendships with non-Muslims, including Christians and Jews (Qur'an 3:28.118), (Qur'an 4:89,101,144), (Qur'an 5:51, 82), even if they are their fathers or relatives (Qur'an 9:23), (Qur'an 58:22). Abu Ubaida was a neighbor who won the praise of the Mohammed, and his father was killed for refusing Islam. Musab Ibn Amir, (one of the first of Mohammed's followers), did not meet with his mother and left her to die because she refused Islam.

The Qur'an teaches racism in that it claims the superiority of Muslims over non-Muslims (Qur'an 3:110.85), (Qur'an 9:28), and insists Islamists treat non-Muslims with disdain, as subhuman, second-class citizens (Qur'an 8:55), (Qur'an 5:59-60), (Qur'an 2:65), (Qur'an 7:166). They are oppressed in Muslim countries, suffering at the hands of Islamists, who have been poisoned with hatred and injustice in the Muslim community. Muslims who impose humiliating tribute on their non-Muslim neighbors do not love them. Love is the essence of life, beginning with the baby in the cradle, then solidified and strengthened by human society. Islam denies the very reality and the essence of love. A Muslim man who is capable of hitting or killing his mother, sister, wife or daughter does not seem to have any love.

Christ called Christians to love one another as He loved them, as it says in the following verse: "So now I am giving you a new commandment: Love each other. Just as I have loved you, you should love each other," John 13:34-35.

In addition, Christ called Christians to love unbelievers and enemies, to pray for them, and to introduce them to the Gospel, as the Bible says in the following verses: "You have heard the law that says, 'Love your neighbor and hate your enemy.' But I say, love your enemies! Pray for those who persecute you! In that way, you will be acting as true children of your Father in heaven. For he gives his sunlight to both the evil and the good, and he sends rain on the just and the unjust alike," Matthew 5:43-45; Luke 6:27-28, 32-33, 35; Romans 12:14. Christianity teaches forgiveness, not retaliation. "Dear friends, never take revenge. Leave that to the righteous anger of God. For the Scriptures say, 'I will take revenge; I will pay them back,' says the Lord. Instead, 'If your enemies are hungry, feed them. If they are thirsty, give them something to drink. In doing this, you will heap burning coals of shame on their heads.'" "Don't let evil conquer you, but conquer evil by doing good," Romans 12:19-21; Matthew 5:38-42.

Islam calls for revenge, as it says in verses 2:178, 194, and 17:33 of the Qur'an.

In ancient times, Moses said to the Jews, "Therefore, love the stranger, for you were strangers in the land of Egypt," Deuteronomy 10:19; Leviticus 19:34.

Sharia Law, an all-encompassing set of restrictions, rules and laws regulating every aspect of Muslim life, also establishes distinct divisions in the Islamic state, encouraging unjust discrimination against women, non-Muslims, and the lower classes. Compensation paid for the death or injury of a victim depends upon that person's religion, class, or sex. For instance, a woman would receive half the compensation paid for a man, compensation for a Jew or Christian would be one-third of that paid for the Muslim, and compensation for certain undesirable races is one-fifteenth the compensation paid for a Muslim. Sharia in some instances protects certain killers from punishment of death. For example, lenience is applied when a Muslim kills a non-Muslim, a Jew or a Christian, or for killing an apostate from Islam. Sharia encourages mistreatment of non-Muslims and protects Muslims from punishment.

Some praise the Islamic law and claim it reflects the highest goals for any society. Further analysis shows the invalidity of this claim and that the law is a huge obstacle for the progress of Islamic countries. Impose Sharia Law and it will infiltrate every aspect of the Muslim way of life, social, cultural, religious, political, and military, and complete control will be exercised over the lives of a Muslim from the cradle to the grave. The Sharia legal system is authoritarian, repressive and brutal, imposed on Muslims in the name of the Islamic god. Muslims then live in bondage to the provisions of the law. At the beginning of the year 900 AD, the law had taken firm hold in its final form. In spite of its stagnant nature and the need for change and evolution, it cannot be modified to conform to the developing values, norms, and humanitarian needs. This is because the Islamists believe the law is divinely inspired, timeless, and relevant.

Islamic law supports and promotes inequality between master and slave, men and women, insured and uninsured. Immoral behavior, ordered or condoned by the brutal laws of Sharia, include child marriage (Qur'an 65:4), common-law marriages, honor killings, female genital mutilation, and polygamy (Qur'an 4:3).

Sharia punishments are unusual and very harsh, and do not allow any room for forgiveness, rehabilitation, or reform. The law requires death for apostates, and those who criticize Mohammed, the Qur'an, or Sharia. It requires the stoning of adulterers, fornicators, and gamblers who drink liquor. Homosexuality is punishable by death and theft requires the cutting off of the perpetrator's hands.

Every Muslim man has authority over other men and women to correct the behavior of his fellow Muslim. Women have authority over other women. Women never have the right to correct a man. Those who assassinate thieves or adulterers or apostates who have left Islam will be pardoned or go unpunished for murder under Islamic law. The law does not punish Muslims who commit crimes of genocide if they repent. Fatwas, orders issued by Islamic clerics to kill apostates, are not binding on the Islamic government, but if an individual Muslim carries them out, there will be no punishment for the crime. Any who disagree with Islam and its laws will be described as enemies of Islam and apostates, and these violators live in fear of vigilante justice by Islamists, who could be anyone, such as friends and neighbors and their relatives, parents, brothers, or sisters.

Civil justice restrictions and limits are misused, and lead to relationships based on fear and arrogance among Muslims. They also lead to a chaotic society, seeing groups of murderers or street mobs take justice into their own hands, punishing women accused of adultery. Boys toss burning acid on girls because they do not like their dress, etc. After turning Muslims against each other, they have to protect the backs of others. Many of the accusations of apostasy and blasphemy are the result of personal grudges against defendants. False accusations are used to settle personal scores or are the means for Islamic governments to silence any opposition, causing deep-seated distrust in the Muslim community. Islam gets its strength from vigilante justice. It is not the power of conviction, but the power of fear.

Sharia Law produces tyranny and dictatorship, and because of the severe nature of the oppressive rules, peaceful coexistence between Islamic Sharia cultures and civilizations of free societies is impossible. There is a fear of mixing with other cultures because non-Islamic Arabs caused destruction of the great ancient civilizations of Egypt and Persia (Qur'an 9:14).

Islam does not allow a Muslim to change religions (Qur'an 9:5.11, 12, 29), (Qur'an 2:217), (Qur'an 4:89), (Qur'an 5:33). This contrasts with the freedom of conscience advocated by Christians (Luke 10:10-12). In Islam, a person born into a Muslim family does not have a choice whether to be a Muslim or not. He is born a Muslim if his parents are Muslims, and this cannot be changed without the risk that person will lose his life. Muslims are not free to leave Islam, a prison for those who wish to leave. Islam has a stranglehold on Muslims from the cradle to the grave. Islam is much harsher than fascism, Nazism, or communism, and has existed much longer than communism and Nazism, because it claims divine authority and superiority.

There is a consensus between all schools of Islamic jurisprudence, including the four main Sunni Muslim groups (al-Maliki, Hannibali, Hanafi, and Shafi'i) as well as Shiites, that any adult male who converts from Islam should be executed if he refuses to return to Islam in a short period of time, usually three days (Qur'an 4:89), (Qur'an 16:106). Opinions differ about whether the female who leaves Islam should be killed or only imprisoned. Islam is the only religion in the world that threatens its followers with death if they try to leave. Therefore, many of the Islamic countries emphasize laws against apostasy from Islam and consider it a crime punishable by death. However, the biggest problem of the Islamic government is that Islamic law gives the right to Muslims to practice vigilante justice and punish Muslim apostates with death, and the killers are assured heavenly rewards for their crimes. Therefore, the biggest threat to the Muslim apostate is that of a relative or friend or other angry Muslim. Authorities often ignore the Islamic attacks on Muslim apostates because they are sympathetic to the offenders. I have followed this problem and, unfortunately, I am seeing it happen with Muslims in the West.

Islamists expand the scope of the definition of "apostate" to include all those who disagree with the beliefs of the "original" Islam. This leaves the door wide open to condemn other Muslims as apostates, deserving of the death penalty. This leads to widespread mistrust and insecurity that torments the Muslim community.

None of the four main Sunni groups are allowed to construct churches or synagogues in villages or cities in the Islamic countries; however, the Hanafi may construct a church or temple, but it must be more than one mile outside the town. The refusal of many Islamic countries to sign the United Nations' Declaration of Human Rights (1948) is because of its insistence on the principle of freedom of religion, where Article 18 states the following: "Everyone has the right to freedom of thought, conscience and religion, and this right includes freedom to change his religion or belief, and freedom to express his belief in teaching, practice, worship and observance, either alone or in community with others."

In retaliation, Islamic organizations around the world push for laws against "defamation of religion" (Islam specifically) in order to suppress and silence objective criticism of Islam. This is not out of commitment to the truth, tolerance, or peace, but out of fear of losing their adherent Muslims. This is what drives the tyrants in the Muslim world to the relentless, violent repression of those they consider bigots.

If a Christian were to blaspheme the Christian religion, they would be expelled from fellowship in the church (1 Timothy 1:13, 14, 20). However, the Bible teaches there is a perpetually open door of repentance in this life on earth, so if he changed his mind and repented, he would be completely forgiven and accepted back into the church.

Prophets of the Bible did not persecute or kill those who opposed and rejected their message. Christians are called to the principle of freedom of conscience: "For you have been called to live in freedom, my brothers and sisters. But don't use your freedom to satisfy your sinful nature. Instead, use your freedom to serve one another in love," Galatians 5:13; 1 Peter 2:16. In fact, Jesus is called the Prince of Peace (Isaiah 9:6). "Blessed are the peacemakers, for they are called sons of God," Matthew 5:9. Jesus did not hate or pressure or threaten any person, enforcing an order to follow Him. He did not have a sword, never killed or ordered the killing anyone. In fact, Jesus advised His followers against using violence when He was arrested in the garden at Gethsemane: "But one of the men with Jesus pulled out his sword and struck the high priest's slave, slashing off his ear. 'Put away your sword,' Jesus told him. 'Those who use the sword will die by the sword,'" Matthew 26:51, 52. The Bible describes the nature of the love of Jesus, saying, "He will not crush the weakest reed or put out a flickering candle..." Matthew 12:20; Isaiah 42:3. Jesus and His disciples preached and were examples of peace (Philippians 4:7; Ephesians 2:17). Before His crucifixion, Jesus Christ assured His disciples, saying, "Peace I leave with you; my peace I give to you. Not as the world gives do I give to you. Let not your hearts be troubled, neither let them be afraid," John 14:27 (ESV).

The lack of freedom of conscience in Islam makes other rights, such as the right to freedom of thought and expression, meaningless. The Qur'an does not encourage Muslims to ask questions (Qur'an 5:101-102); in fact, Mohammed urged his followers to kill Muslims to silence his critics. Objective criticism of Mohammed or the Qur'an on the basis of historical documents offends Islamists, and Islamic organizations are given leeway to prevent any criticism of Islam, claiming it is insulting and offensive. This trick is practiced in many societies and civilized governments, insisting that any criticism, even objectively honest, is an insult to them in order to punish and silence the source. There is no accepting responsibility for the crimes committed by Islamist militants; instead blame is placed elsewhere. They assert that Islam is always innocent, no matter how clear the evidence to the contrary, allowing only those statements that could bring praise to Islam, and hiding and covering up those bringing shame. This prevents the light of truth, closing all the doors and windows around the Muslim mind. The widespread killing of apostates and critics of Islam in prisons at large results in frightened followers of Islam, not believers. To be a committed Muslim, a person must adhere to a relationship, not with the god of Islam, but with the Islamic state and the laws governing it.

Whenever there is criticism of the Qur'an and the prophet, imams begin issuing death fatwas that allow Muslims to kill the source of the criticism. Devastating, violent riots ensue in Islamic countries amid rising cries to restrict freedom of thought in order to prevent criticism of Islam in the West or anywhere.

Restriction of free thought and questioning has led to the paralysis of the Islamic mind, destroying initiative and innovation. Any followers of the intellectual type are under tight control to prohibit questioning, using concern for their security and survival as an excuse to retain all developing innovation and discovery for the Islamic cause. Islamists are trained to never doubt, and not to criticize the Qur'an or Sharia; instead, to blame the dysfunctional aspects of the Muslim community on external factors, such as foreign influence.

Muslims suffer disproportionately from the rule of tyrants, while Islam insists that the ruling ideology of the state gives political and humanitarian rights. Islamic law, which developed more than 1,400 years ago, is against democracy. It is based on the will of their god, according to interpretation by Islamists of popular sovereignty, and encourages bloody jihad to impose Islam on others and for the expansion of its borders. It imposes the death penalty for blasphemy (criticism of Islam) and apostasy (leaving Islam). The roots of these basic ideas of inequality abound in Islamic cultures. And, so, democracy is contrary to the principle of the supremacy of Islam, and cannot coexist in the same country for long. Democracy requires fundamental freedoms of thought, conscience, religion, and expression. A democracy operates on cash or fair exchange, encourages debate, the reconciliation of opposing views and compromise, concepts completely alien to the Islamic totalitarian theocracy. Democracy is the rule of the people, while Sharia is the alleged judgment of the Islamic god.

The main purpose of Islam is to establish a theocratic state ruled by a totalitarian Islamic law based on the ideology of

Islam. Democracy contradicts this. Islamic law protects Muslims in leadership accused of committing serious crimes such as murder, adultery, theft, rape, etc. Sharia considers revolt against the Caliph (an Islamic ruler), a serious crime, even if the ruler is unfair. Repeal of the law protecting the Muslim ruler can only occur upon leaving Islam or if it goes against the provisions of the law. In this case, requiring his subjects to overthrow or assassinate him.

The powerful Islamist movement seeks to create a theocratic authoritarian regime hostile to democracy. First established in the history of Medina in the seventh century with Mohammed, the prophet of Islam, as its leader, it has become the model theocracy that leaders are trying to impose. There is no separation between religion and state in Islam, which is a basic necessity in a democracy. This leads to the persecution of minorities and dissidents and stifles freedom of conscience. In an Islamic theocracy, the Islamic god is the absolute ruler who cannot be opposed or even discussed. God judges by the ruling Islamic Muslim Caliph who is his shadow on the ground. Therefore, it is the religious duty to blindly obey. Anyone who rebels against Islam, rebels against their god (Qur'an 4:59, 83). An Islamic caliphate is not ruler according to elected or appointed authority, instead counting on heritage and loyalty of traditional allegiance, which leads to a mock election. There are no legislative tasks in the Islamic state, and therefore, no need for democratic legislatures. These are not the principles of democracy.

Islamists denounce democracy and describe it as anti-Islamic. Hassan al-Banna, the founder of the Muslim Brotherhood, considered democracy a betrayal of Islamic values. However, Islamists have used elections to gain power. The Islamist movement Hamas has won in the elections in Gaza in

2006. Like the communists do, Islamists take over elections, and democracy is terminated. Islamists constitute the largest power in the anti-democratic world.

Unlike Islam, Christianity is not a political, religious system. Jesus Christ rejected being forced to take on the role of earthly king, as the Bible says in John 6:15, "Perceiving then that they were about to come and take him by force to make him king, Jesus withdrew again to the mountain by himself." "Jesus answered, 'My kingdom is not of this world. If my kingdom were of this world, my servants would have been fighting, that I might not be delivered over to the Jews. But my kingdom is not from the world,'" John 18:36. "...Therefore render to Caesar the things that are Caesar's, and to God the things that are God's," Matthew 22:21. Christianity teaches the separation of church and state. Although this doesn't mean God should be removed from the citizen's lives but that the citizens are not forced to adhere to one specific religion, are not ruled by religion.

Although Mohammed slightly improved the status of women in his day and promoted helping widows, the improvements were limited and inadequate, because Islam does not protect women from abuse and persecution in conservative Muslim societies. Women in Islam are considered property owned by the man, and are regarded as inferior to men, as noted in the Qur'an, verses 2:228 and 4:34.

1. Women are under the control of male relatives until they become the property of their husband, who is chosen or approved by her parents. Women are regarded as something owned by the man. This may be her father or her brother until taken in marriage, when she would become her husband's property (Qur'an 3:14). Therefore, financial independence and sexual freedom is impossible

for women in Islam. Her guardian prevents a woman from receiving an education, and does not allow her to travel, work, or leave the house without being in the company of her husband or a male relative, unless the travel is mandatory, such as the Hajj.

2. The god of Islam recommends wife beating for a variety of reasons (Qur'an 4:34). In addition, The Qur'an allows a Muslim man to punish his wife by withholding marital relations with her for four months (Qur'an 4:34), (Qur'an 2:226). However, the Muslim wife who seeks to settle marital disputes in negotiations with her husband is considered rebellious (Qur'an 4:128). There is a clear double standard when it comes to the treatment of women.

3. Upon the birth of a child, a sacrifice is required. If the baby is a boy, two sheep or two goats are required, but if the child is female, only one sheep or goat must be sacrificed.

4. Women can inherit only half of what her brother, husband, or son would receive (Qur'an 4:11, 176). Women also may not partake in the spoils of war.

5. In a Sharia court, the testimony of two women is required to equal the value of one man's testimony (Qur'an 2:282). The general rule is to not accept the testimony of a woman in the important issues.

6. If a woman were killed, the compensation would be half the compensation for a slain man.

7. A Muslim girl's family who follows the Shafi'i School of the law could be forced to perform female circumcision on her at an early age. Female circumcision is a process of female genital mutilation.

8. Islam permits the marriage of young girls to older men. Islam allows this under the pretext of not violating the sanctity of marriage (Qur'an 65:4). Mohammed married a child daughter of his friend, Aisha, when she was only seven years old, then consummated the marriage when she was just nine.

9. A Muslim wife is her husband's property and a means of sexual pleasure (Qur'an 2:223), (Qur'an 33:50), (Qur'an 4:3.24), and he may have as many additional women as he wishes (prisoners of war, slaves, and concubines). Muslim men can marry up to four wives then divorce one and replace her with another (Qur'an 4:20). This harem type system is basically domestic servitude. Islam completely ignores the immorality of polygamy and has no respect for the feelings of women.

10. In Islam, men can divorce their wives for any reason (Qur'an 66:5), and all that is required is the husband saying three times, "I divorce you," according to the Qur'an, verses 2:226-232. A woman does not have this same right.

11. Mohammed taught that women are inferior in intelligence and religion.

12. Sharia imposes a set of tougher, repressive laws relating to

women wherever strict Islamic law applies. For example, they are forced to wear the hijab (veil) (Qur'an 33:59.33), (Qur'an 24:31.58), and are prevented the opportunity for education, etc. Muslim women are required to cover the entire body except for her eyes, her wrists, and feet, with the veil. The veil is a symbol of isolation, oppression, and repression, making the Muslim woman look like a ghost of the dead and declaring her part of a debased level in society.

13. Sharia treats rape victims in a very unfair manner. In order to prove rape, there must be four witnesses to testify against the man (Qur'an 24:4). The woman's testimony, as the victim, is not acceptable by itself. This makes it impossible for a woman to prove rape, which then makes her vulnerable to becoming the victim of honor killing, or of stoning, by virtue of Islamic law for committing adultery or premarital sex. Even if found guilty of rape, the rapist can eliminate the punishment by making payment of the bride price to marry her.

14. The Qur'an teaches that women are unclean by nature and the man who touches her before prayer is also considered unclean, even if she is his wife (Qur'an 4:43), (Qur'an 5:6). If you walk a dog or a donkey or a woman in front of a praying man, his prayer is canceled, and he must begin his prayer again. Women are considered unclean during the monthly menstrual period and cannot pray or fast in those days.

If honor and respect for a woman exists in an Islamic family, it is in spite of the teachings of Islam, not because of it. Christian teachings relating to women contradict the teachings of Islam dramatically. Christianity teaches that men and women are equal before God: "There is neither Jew nor Greek, there is neither slave nor free, there is no male and female, for you are all one in Christ Jesus," Galatians 3:28; Colossians 3:11. Christ praised women for their faith (Luke 21:1-4; Matthew 15:28). He healed them (Mark 5:21-34), and cast demons out of them (Luke 8:1-3; 13:10-13). He also forgave (John 4:1-42; 8:3-11; Luke 7:36-50), and blessed them (Luke 7:50).

Many of the people in Christianity most respected for their holiness were women, including the Blessed Virgin Mary, Mother of Jesus. The first Christian missionary sent out by Jesus Himself was a Samaritan woman (John 4:5-43). The first person who saw and talked with Jesus after His resurrection from the dead was a woman, Mary Magdalene (John 20:11-18). He did not even consider that touching a woman would defile Him; instead, He modeled freedom from those stereotypes and the old laws of inequality.

The god of Mohammed encourages polygamy (Qur'an 66:1.5). A wife cannot prevent her husband from taking other wives. She has no say in the matter. In Islam, the marital relationship is an exploitative relationship for the benefit of the man. Polygamy causes instability of the family and gender inequality. The Qur'an tells the wife that they can be replaced (Qur'an 66:5), (Qur'an 4:20), making Islamic marriage unstable and unsafe. Some Muslim wives try to have more children in order to prevent their husbands from marrying other women, knowing they will not be able survive on their own. Polygamy destroys the family, which is the basis of society. It leads to high proliferation rates and poverty. This is a method used to increase the population of Muslims, not only because the man begets children from several wives, but also because the wife worries about the stability of the marriage to her husband, so carries the burden of creating a large family, hoping he doesn't take additional wives.

The Qur'an (Qur'an 4:3) does not allow more than four wives for a Muslim man at one time. Slaves, prisoners of war and devout Muslim women gave themselves to Mohammed, so he claimed that he received a message from his god exempting him from the law (Qur'an 33:50), that he was allowed to marry any number of women, as well as taking slaves and concubines. In the end Mohammed had taken thirteen wives as well as many concubines.

In addition to the four legal wives allowed by the Qur'an (Qur'an 33:50), (Qur'an 0.4:3.24), a Muslim man is permitted as many women as he wants in the form of prisoners of war, slaves, and concubines. As mentioned before, a man can marry more than four wives if he divorces one and replaces her with another (Qur'an 4:20). The Qur'an's permitting of polygamy despises the women's rights, creating a family bondage. A Muslim husband is required by law to rectify the wrongs to all of his wives, but this is just about financial support and time spent with each of them (Qur'an 4:3). He is not required to impart equal passion towards each of his wives (Qur'an 4:129). Mohammed himself was biased in his emotions towards his wives, Aisha being the one he loved more than the other wives.

Polygamy is the cause of most of the resentment, hatred and misery in the Muslim family. Polygamy disperses and tears the Muslim family apart, each wife becoming an autonomous center of power within the family, leading to fierce competition, hostility, and antagonism. Children grow up in this poisoned atmosphere of quarreling and insults, making them look negatively on life, hating their father and his other wives who cause them problems. Each mother tries to protect her children's birthrights and relationship with their father, but usually they end up feeling neglected. The extra special treatment then given by the mother often leads to pampered, arrogant children. The fear of polygamy among Muslim women causes a deep-rooted bitterness even in happy marriages that are monogamous.

Islamic law prohibits Muslim women from marrying non-Muslim men (Qur'an 2:221), but allows Muslim men to marry non-Muslim women (Qur'an 5:5). This means that all children of mixed marriages will be Muslim. This is one of the aspects of Islamic law which is biased against women.

Muslim women are afraid of their husbands, and will not involve the police when her husband beats her in an Islamic country. They have no choice but to accept the humiliation if he decides to take other wives. There is no freedom to complain to the media, local or foreign, because this is a rebellion against Islam itself and is severely punished by the sword of Islamic law.

The God of the Bible designed marriage to be a monogamous relationship. God created only one woman, Eve, for one man, Adam, in the beginning (Genesis 2:24; Matthew 19:5-6; Mark 10:7-8). Although God has allowed polygamy in ancient times, He did not encourage it (Malachi 2:13-15). Most of the major prophets of God (Moses, Jeremiah, Ezekiel, etc.) took only one wife, and some of them remained celibate (Elijah, Elisha). Jesus did not marry at all. Christianity emphasizes monogamy (Matthew 19:4-5; 1 Corinthians 7:2), requires its leaders to exercise monogamy (1 Timothy 3:2-3, 12; Titus 1:6), and teaches that the wife is an equal partner with her husband.

Christian marriage is given high spiritual status and divorce is restricted. The God of the Bible hates divorce (Malachi 2:16), and there are only certain circumstances in which divorce is allowed, such as adultery or abandonment. The Christian husband is not to abuse his wife in any way, for the husband is commanded to love his wife as Christ loves the church, and sacrificed His life for it. The wife must respect her husband and accept his loving leadership (Ephesians 5:22-33; 1 Peter 3:7; 1 Corinthians 7:14, 23; Colossians 3:19).

Christianity teaches that marriage is a sacred tradition, a linking of lives blessed by God. It unites a man and his wife in one family (Ephesians 5:31; Genesis 2:24). The marriage ceremony is a sacred rite performed by a priest in the church. The bride and groom exchange pledges to fulfill the marriage vows of love and dignity in a covenant of holy matrimony, blessed by God. It is a new beginning for the couple, as they are united in wedlock for life, a commitment that ends only upon death.

There is a major difference between Islamic and Christian holidays. Celebrating Christian holidays is commemorating the divine intervention for the salvation of mankind. Christmas is the holiday celebrating the birth of Jesus Christ, the Savior of mankind. Easter celebrates the resurrection of Jesus Christ in His victory over death, which completes the work of salvation on the cross. Both Christians and Jews celebrate Passover because of God's promise to save the firstborn of the children of Israel from death.

In Islam, the Eid (festival or holy day) symbols the end of the fasting month "Ramadan," ending the period of the Muslim personal sacrificial fast. Pena celebrates the anniversary of Islamic human achievements. Also, Eid al-Adha, which comes seventy days after Ramadan, celebrates the willingness of Abraham to sacrifice his son "Ishmael."

Chapter V
Of the State of War & Peace

The historical process of the Islamic Movement saw violence emerge as a foundational attribute when it entered into a phase of conflict, establishing its authority and sovereignty over the tribes of the "Hijaz." Later, after the death of Mohammed, with the expansion of the Islamic movement on the Arabian Peninsula and substantive developments that allowed the pursuit of this expansion outside the Arabian Peninsula, it became apparent that the spread of Islam by combat was possible. This ideology was religious in nature and was documented in correlation with more and more violence.

The Islamic mind is not able to distinguish amongst the violence in society, going through stages of evolution and the way it fit the time with respect to the evolutionary nature of the movement to the state, but the leaders of Islam did not expect the people to come to hate the violence. This is what characterized the violence in Islam, making it Holy, emerging from the process of invasion in the desert environment. That is why the sacred texts that we have give the advantage of justifying this historic process, as it says in verse 3:110 of the Qur'an: "You are the best nation produced for mankind. You enjoin what is right and forbid what is wrong and believe in Allah. If only the People of the Scripture had believed, it would have been better for them. Among them are believers, but most of them are defiantly reprobates."

This historical background has made Islam emphasize the duty to Islamize of the world, and stresses the inevitability of the final victory of Islam at the end of the world. Islam presented the idea of jihad as a justification to spread the ideology to the Bedouin. This is what establishes the Muslim jihadist mentality, justifying the act, no matter that it was gained from violence.

The philosophical and mystical currents, which played a role in the intellectual life of Muslim countries, have eased away from this violent tendency outwardly, but the principle of violence has not been removed from the system of Islam. This sacred principle remains active, thus in the intellectual structure of Islam there is a constant incitement to violence, making it morally acceptable.

Mohammed called on Muslims to treat each other as brothers in verse 3:103 of the Qur'an: "And hold firmly to the rope of Allah all together and do not become divided. And remember the favor of Allah upon you—when you were enemies and He brought your hearts together and you became, by His favor, brothers." He also urged them to reject friendships with non-Muslims in verse 3:28: "Let not believers take infidels as allies rather than believers."

"O you, who have believed, do not take the Jews and the Christians as allies. They are in fact allies of one another," Qur'an, verse 5:51.

"O you who have believed, do not take My enemies and your enemies as allies, extending to them affection while they have disbelieved in what came to you of the truth, having driven out the Prophet and yourselves only because you believe in Allah, your Lord. If you have come out for jihad in My cause and seeking means to My approval, take them not as friends. You confide to them affection, but I am most knowing of what you have concealed and what you have declared. And whoever does it among you has certainly strayed from the soundness of the way," Qur'an, verse 60:1.

Muslims are instructed to participate in holy war (jihad) and the killing of non-believers, if necessary, in order to force them to accept Islam (Qur'an 9:5.29); also, as it says in verse 2:193: "Fight them until there is no more fitnah and [until] worship is acknowledged to be for Allah."

In Islam, a Muslim who falls who falls on the battlefield is encouraged to kill as many non-believers as possible before falling. Mohammed distributed rewards and sanctioned his followers, urging them to follow his example.

Islam supports and encourages the violence of fanatical Muslims, urging them to spread Islam by force, conquering non-Muslims in every nation. Mohammed said, "I ordered to fight the people until they say there is no god but Allah" (Bukhari, Jihad). Jihad is a religious duty for Muslims, similar to the Hajj. Rejection of the doctrine of jihad is to reject a Qur'anic essential, one occupying a high rank of importance in Islam. Verses abound in the Qur'an, calling for jihad and to kill infidels who reject Islam and apostates who leave Islam, a call for an open and global jihad (Qur'an 2:193).

"Indeed, the penalty for those who wage war against Allah and his messenger and strive upon earth [to cause] corruption is none but that they be killed or crucified or that their hands and feet be cut off from opposite sides or that they be exiled from the land. That is for them a disgrace in this world; and for them in the Hereafter is a great punishment," the Qur'an, verses 5:33, 51.

"So when you meet those who disbelieve (non-Muslims) in battle, strike their necks until, when you have inflicted slaughter upon them, then secure their bonds, and either confer favor afterwards or ransom them until the war lays down its burdens. That is the command. And if Allah had willed, He could have taken vengeance upon them Himself, but He ordered armed struggle to test some of you by means of others. And those who are killed in the cause of Allah—never will He waste their deeds," the Qur'an, verse 47:4.

While war is the exception to the rule in the history of most civilized nations, it is the norm in the Islamic culture. Jihad is a basic principle of Islam, not just a chance happening in Islamic history. There is a long, bloody history of Islam reflecting these teachings, packed with relentless harassment, persecution, oppression, and killing of non-Muslims. All the battles were offensive, aggressive battles with the exception of Mohammed, which was defensive.

The Qur'an ensures that a Muslim who kills in Islamic Jihad for the god of Mohammed, will be greatly rewarded in a heaven teeming with food, drink, and women (Qur'an 55:46-78).

"Indeed, Allah has purchased from the believers their lives and their properties in exchange for that they will have Paradise. They fight in the cause of Allah, so they kill and are killed. It is a true promise [binding] upon Him in the Torah and the Gospel and the Qur'an. And who is truer to his covenant than Allah? So rejoice in your transaction, which you have contracted. And it is that which is the great attainment," the Qur'an, verse 9:111.

Mohammed said, "Know that Paradise is under the shades of swords" (Bukhari, Jihad). Mohammed promised these bonuses, which are nothing but a desert mirage, in order to motivate his fighters. What he was able to give them a reason to live, gave them a reason to die.

The word "jihad" in its various forms is discussed about thirty-five times in the Qur'an: almost nine times in the Mecca verses, and approximately twenty-six times in the Medina verses. The verb "kill" is used in more 123 different instances. The abundant use of these words in the Qur'an reflects the substantial growth of Mohammed's military force after immigrating to Medina. Few of the use of these words are used in a context outside of the military. Only ten times is "kill" used in context of war.

Islam is not a religion of peace. It is the only religion in the world today that calls for violence against non-Muslims, inciting its followers to engage in "jihad" (holy war). There are contradictions in the Qur'an, which may be the reason people promote it as a peaceful religion. The Qur'an contains an entire chapter (surah) on the spoils of war, called Al-Anfal 8. There is no doubt about the immoral motives in the historical record of Mohammed, the prophet of Islam, but his followers claim that he may have inadvertently presented a literal concept of jihad, not the spiritual concept as he intended, as it says in verse 4:95 of the Qur'an:

"Not equal are those believers remaining at home—other than the disabled—and the mujahideen, who strive and fight in the cause of Allah with their wealth and their lives. Allah has preferred the mujahideen through their wealth and their lives over those who remain behind, by degrees. And to both Allah has promised the best reward. But Allah has preferred the mujahideen over those who remain behind with a great reward—"

And in the Qur'an, verse 8:65: "O Prophet, urge the believers to battle. If there are among you twenty who are steadfast, they will overcome two hundred. And if there are among you one hundred who are steadfast, they will overcome a thousand of those who have disbelieved because they are a people who do not understand."

In contrast, the Bible contains about 420 verses on the subject of peace; a condition man has sought since ancient times. However, deep inner peace is a gift from the living God to the human soul; something man cannot achieve for himself.

"How beautiful on the mountains are the feet of the

messenger who brings good news, the good news of peace and salvation, the news that the God of Israel reigns!" Isaiah 52:7.

"The peace of God, which surpasses all understanding, will guard your hearts and minds in Christ Jesus," Philippians 4:7 (ESV).

"Then you will experience God's peace, which exceeds anything we can understand. His peace will guard your hearts and minds as you live in Christ Jesus," Philippians 4:7 (NLT).

"For God is not a God of disorder but of peace, as in all the meetings of God's holy people," 1 Corinthians 14:33.

"For the Kingdom of God is not a matter of what we eat or drink, but of living a life of goodness and peace and joy in the Holy Spirit," Romans 14:17.

"God blesses those who work for peace, for they will be called the children of God," Matthew 5:9.

Conclusion

Anyone who goes deep in the Islamic ocean will realize sooner or later the imperfection of it. For god to be GOD, he has to be perfect, faultless, and pure. Perfection is an absolute virtue of a Holy God. The Qur'anic discourse has a strange way of randomly changing, causing confusion and an inability for its followers to feel confident. This is because of its source. Only unmarred perfection should come from a Holy God, because His nature is spotless and supreme and there is no way to have confidence in a god who is not perfect, who changes his mind, and who lies and deceives. It is not possible for God to be a liar, because He would have no righteous morality, the aspect of perfection in Himself would fail. Followers of Islam who examine the Qur'an instead of blindly following will see the imperfection and will have serious doubts about the teachings of Mohammed. The Qur'an as a constitution, a chart of life, fails because it is an imperfect word given by an imperfect god, demanding its believers follow along without question.

It takes only a small effort to research history and learn Mohammed's tribe was known as traders of religion. While traveling Iraq, Syria, Greece, and Turkey a pagan man would be the one to go between the tribe and the local people, learning about their beliefs and practices. The tribe would then combine the local religion with Islamic teachings to make it more commercially acceptable. This, combined with the use of the sword, caused its rapid spread.

The dialogue between the Islamic god and Muslim men, granting them women, was a very important aspect of the reward system promised to faithful men. In this pagan world, sex was at the forefront of society in that era. Believers were also promised a paradise filled with clear, flowing water and honey. These items were scarce in the region of the Arabian Peninsula because of the arid desert conditions, and so were unimaginable and something desired by the desert people around Mecca. This is one of many examples of text taken from the Bible and restructured to fit Mohammed's teachings. The people's ignorance caused them to believe the horizon was their limit. Because they had no means to travel outside the general vicinity, they blindly believed the stories of Mohammed. The use of fear and reward, as a system of religious discipline, laid the groundwork for the future all-encompassing takeover of Islam.

Islamic faith is a combination of blind submission, mimicry of belief and exaggeration to penetrate the mind's ability to understand and grasp the qualities of god. With the technological advances and the ability to travel easily from nation to nation, it would seem the tight hold Islamic teaching had on the tribes in the time of Mohammed would be loosening. However, that is not the case. The religion keeps being reinvented as necessary to accommodate the changing times, but the foundational teachings of the Qur'an are not adequate or suitable for the twenty-first century.

Sources and References

Many of the following materials are from Arabic resources which have not been translated.

1- The Holy Bible
2- Qur'an, quran.com
3- Sahih Al-Bokarhi
4- Sahih Muslims
5- Ibn-Majah
6- Al-Tormothi
7- Ibn Elzimlkani, Clarification on the Science of the Qur'an.
8- Al-Taalbei, Philology and the Secret of Arabian Language.
9- Literature writer, Ibn Qutaiba
10- Concise Arabic Encyclopedia, Dar Al-sha'ab, Cairo, Egypt, illustrated edition, 1961. Abn Al-atheer, Abu al-Hasan Ali ibn Abi al-kerem, the full of history, The House of the Arabian Book, auditing, Sheikh Abdul Wahab al-Najjar, Beirut, 4th addition, 1983 AD.
11- Ibn Khaldun, Abu Zaid Abdul Rahman Moroccan, Book Lessons and the Office Debutante and the News in the Days of the Arabs and non-Arabs and Berbers, the school library, the House of Lebanon Books, Beirut, 1961 AD.
12- Ibn Hisham, Abu Muhammad Abdullah, the biography of the Prophet, Dar Rihani for printing and publishing, Beirut.
13- Ibn Al-atheer, The End, on the strange talk of the Hadeath.
14- Al-Jabri, Mohammed Abed, Configure the Arab Mind, Center for Arab Unity Studies, Beirut, 1988 AD.
15- Abe Ali Alqala, Anecdotes.

16- Al-Suyuti, Jalal al-Din, History of the Caliphs, examined by Sheikh Qasim Achamma'a Al-Rifai and Sheikh Mohammed Ottoman, Dar-Alqalem, Beirut, 1986.
17- Tabari, Abu Ja'far Muhammad ibn Jarir al-Tabari, the History of Tabari (Nations and Kings), Volume I: pre-date of Prophet Muhammad, 1987 AD.
18- Ali, Jawad, Details in the History of the Arabs before Islam, Dar Al-aeilm, Beirut, May 1968.
19- Ibn-Sekiet, Repair the Logic to Fine-tune the Wordy.
20- Masoudi, Abou El Hassan Ali bin Hussein bin Ali, Meadows of Gold, and Essence of Metals, Scientific Library, Beirut, 1986 AD.
21- Waaqidi, Mohammed bin Omar bin Waaqid, Book of Magazi, examined by Dr. Marsden Jones, the world of books, Beirut, 1984 AD.
22- Basra and Khoffa, Abu Al-barakat Abdulrahman bin Mohammed Al-Anbarai, Fairness of Disagreement Matters Between Grammarians.
23- Abu Bakr Ibn Abdulrahman Abdalqahir Al-Jerjani, The Signs of Miracles.
24- Al-zaja'aj, Expressions of the Qur'an and Clarification to the Ills.
25- Zmkhcri, The Basis of Rhetoric.
26- Khaza'al Al-Majidi, The Canaanite gods, published in Baghdad 1987.
27- Khaza'al Al-Majidi, The Religions and Belief of the Pre-history, Published by Dar Al- Shorooq, 1997.

About the Author

Born as a Muslim in Iraq, Michael Paul set out to prove himself worthy of his religion, only to find emptiness and questions in need of answers no one seemed able to give him. Because he was considered a rebel for serving the U.S. military during Operation Iraqi Freedom and for going against his culture's traditional religion, he paid a heavy price. He was persecuted, then eventually fled his family, and over the next few years survived events most people in the West, who believe in freedom, could not even imagine. He was kidnapped multiple times and tortured, including being held, hung by his hands, which were tied behind his back, while being beaten nearly to death. He hid, homeless and starving, to avoid being captured and killed. Thankfully, because of his proud service to the American troops as an Arab/English Interpreter and Cultural Advisor, he was granted the opportunity to immigrate to the United States.

He now resides in north Idaho where he is pursuing his master's degree and plans to go on to achieve his PhD. Michael Paul established and acts as President and CEO of the ministry, Salvation For Muslims. He has spoken at numerous churches, on College and University campuses, at conferences for evangelizing Muslims, at Ground Zero, and on television and radio. He teaches evangelical workshops, and a series on Islam, the Qur'an, and Muslim culture and faith. Look for his first book, *Underground*, a collection written while he was in hiding in the Middle East, waiting to escape to America.

* * *

The editor, Lisa J. Lickel, writes best-selling inspirational fiction and is a freelance editor whose clients have won numerous awards. Visit LisaLickel.com for more information.

www.ingramcontent.com/pod-product-compliance
Lightning Source LLC
Chambersburg PA
CBHW070800050426
42452CB00012B/2420